TODAY CARD

QUESTION: _____

or choose:

What do I need to know today?   How can I improve today?
Where should I focus my energy?   Who is affecting me?

INITIAL READING:

_____
_____

DAY'S REFLECTION:

_____
_____

TODAY'S CARD: _____

DATE: _/_/_

QUESTION: _____

or choose: _____

What do I need to know today?   How can I improve today?
Where should I focus my energy?   Who is affecting me?

INITIAL READING:

_____
_____
_____

DAY'S REFLECTION:

_____
_____

TODAY'S CARD: _____

DATE: __/__/__

QUESTION: _____

or choose: _____

What do I need to know today?   How can I improve today?
Where should I focus my energy? Who is affecting me?

INITIAL READING:

_____
_____
_____

DAY'S REFLECTION:

_____
_____

TODAY'S CARD: _____

DATE: / /

QUESTION: _____

or choose:

What do I need to know today?   How can I improve today?
Where should I focus my energy?   Who is affecting me?

INITIAL READING:

_____

_____

DAY'S REFLECTION:

_____

_____

TODAY'S CARD: _____

DATE: __/__

QUESTION: _____

or choose:

What do I need to know today?   How can I improve today?
Where should I focus my energy?   Who is affecting me?

INITIAL READING:

_____

_____

_____

DAY'S REFLECTION:

_____

_____

TODAY'S CARD: _____

DATE: __/__

QUESTION: _____

or choose:

What do I need to know today? How can I improve today?
Where should I focus my energy? Who is affecting me?

INITIAL READING:

_____
_____
_____

DAY'S REFLECTION:

_____
_____

TODAY'S CARD: _____

DATE: __/__/__

QUESTION: _____

or choose: _____

What do I need to know today?   How can I improve today?
Where should I focus my energy?   Who is affecting me?

INITIAL READING:

_____
_____
_____

DAY'S REFLECTION:

_____
_____

TODAY'S CARD: _____

DATE: __/__

QUESTION: _____

or choose: _____

What do I need to know today?   How can I improve today?
Where should I focus my energy?   Who is affecting me?

INITIAL READING:

_____

_____

_____

DAY'S REFLECTION:

_____

_____

TODAY'S CARD: _____

DATE: / /

QUESTION: _____

or choose: _____

What do I need to know today?   How can I improve today?
Where should I focus my energy?   Who is affecting me?

INITIAL READING:

_____
_____
_____

DAY'S REFLECTION:

_____
_____

TODAY'S CARD: _____

DATE: __/__

QUESTION: _____

or choose: _____

What do I need to know today?   How can I improve today?
Where should I focus my energy?   Who is affecting me?

INITIAL READING:

_____
_____
_____

DAY'S REFLECTION:

_____
_____

TODAY'S CARD: _____

DATE: _/_/_

QUESTION: _____

or choose: _____

What do I need to know today?   How can I improve today?
Where should I focus my energy?   Who is affecting me?

INITIAL READING:

_____
_____
_____

DAY'S REFLECTION:

_____
_____

TODAY'S CARD: _____

DATE: / /

QUESTION: _____

or choose: _____

What do I need to know today? How can I improve today?
Where should I focus my energy? Who is affecting me?

INITIAL READING:

_____

_____

DAY'S REFLECTION:

_____

_____

TODAY'S CARD: _____

DATE: _/_/_

QUESTION: _____

or choose: _____

What do I need to know today?   How can I improve today?
Where should I focus my energy?   Who is affecting me?

INITIAL READING:

_____
_____
_____

DAY'S REFLECTION:

_____
_____

TODAY'S CARD: _____

DATE: _/_/_

QUESTION: _____

or choose: _____

What do I need to know today?   How can I improve today?
Where should I focus my energy?   Who is affecting me?

INITIAL READING:

_____

_____

DAY'S REFLECTION:

_____

_____

TODAY'S CARD: _____

QUESTION: _____

or choose: _____

What do I need to know today?   How can I improve today?
Where should I focus my energy? Who is affecting me?

INITIAL READING:

_____
_____
_____

DAY'S REFLECTION:

_____
_____

DATE: / /

TODAY'S CARD: _____

DATE: _/_/_

QUESTION: _____

or choose: _____

What do I need to know today? How can I improve today?
Where should I focus my energy? Who is affecting me?

INITIAL READING:

_____

_____

_____

DAY'S REFLECTION:

_____

_____

TODAY'S CARD: _____

DATE: / /

QUESTION: _____
_____

or choose:

What do I need to know today?   How can I improve today?
Where should I focus my energy?   Who is affecting me?

INITIAL READING:

_____
_____
_____

DAY'S REFLECTION:

_____
_____

TODAY'S CARD: _____

DATE: _/_/_

QUESTION: _____

or choose: _____

What do I need to know today? How can I improve today?
Where should I focus my energy? Who is affecting me?

INITIAL READING:

_____

_____

DAY'S REFLECTION:

_____

_____

TODAY'S CARD: _____

DATE: __/__/__

QUESTION: _____

or choose:

What do I need to know today? How can I improve today?
Where should I focus my energy? Who is affecting me?

INITIAL READING:

_____
_____
_____

DAY'S REFLECTION:

_____
_____

TODAY'S CARD: _____

DATE: __/__

QUESTION: _____

or choose: _____

What do I need to know today?   How can I improve today?
Where should I focus my energy?   Who is affecting me?

INITIAL READING:

_____
_____
_____

DAY'S REFLECTION:

_____
_____

TODAY'S CARD: _____

DATE: 4/4

QUESTION: _____

or choose: _____

What do I need to know today?   How can I improve today?
Where should I focus my energy?   Who is affecting me?

INITIAL READING:

_____
_____
_____

DAY'S REFLECTION:

_____
_____

TODAY'S CARD: _____

DATE: _/_/_

QUESTION: _____

or choose: _____

What do I need to know today?   How can I improve today?
Where should I focus my energy?   Who is affecting me?

INITIAL READING:

_____
_____
_____

DAY'S REFLECTION:

_____
_____

TODAY'S CARD: _____

DATE: _/_/_

QUESTION: _____

or choose: _____

What do I need to know today?   How can I improve today?
Where should I focus my energy?   Who is affecting me?

INITIAL READING:

_____
_____
_____

DAY'S REFLECTION:

_____
_____

TODAY'S CARD: _____ DATE: _/_/_

QUESTION: _____

or choose: _____

What do I need to know today?   How can I improve today?
Where should I focus my energy?   Who is affecting me?

INITIAL READING:

_____
_____
_____

DAY'S REFLECTION:

_____
_____

TODAY'S CARD: _____

DATE: _/_/_

QUESTION: _____

or choose: _____

What do I need to know today?   How can I improve today?
Where should I focus my energy?   Who is affecting me?

INITIAL READING:

_____
_____
_____

DAY'S REFLECTION:

_____
_____

TODAY'S CARD: _____

QUESTION: _____

or choose: _____

What do I need to know today?   How can I improve today?
Where should I focus my energy?   Who is affecting me?

INITIAL READING:

_____
_____
_____

DAY'S REFLECTION:

_____
_____

DATE: _____

TODAY'S CARD: _____

DATE: __/__

QUESTION: _____

or choose:

What do I need to know today?   How can I improve today?
Where should I focus my energy?   Who is affecting me?

INITIAL READING:

_____
_____
_____

DAY'S REFLECTION:

_____
_____

TODAY'S CARD: _____

DATE: / /

QUESTION: _____

or choose:

What do I need to know today?   How can I improve today?
Where should I focus my energy?   Who is affecting me?

INITIAL READING:

_____

_____

DAY'S REFLECTION:

_____

_____

TODAY'S CARD: _____

DATE: _/_/_

QUESTION: _____

or choose: _____

What do I need to know today?   How can I improve today?
Where should I focus my energy?   Who is affecting me?

INITIAL READING:

_____
_____
_____

DAY'S REFLECTION:

_____
_____

TODAY'S CARD: _____

QUESTION: _____

or choose: _____

What do I need to know today? How can I improve today?
Where should I focus my energy? Who is affecting me?

INITIAL READING:

_____
_____
_____

DAY'S REFLECTION:

_____
_____

DATE: __/__

TODAY'S CARD: _____

DATE: __/__

QUESTION: _____

or choose:

What do I need to know today?   How can I improve today?
Where should I focus my energy? Who is affecting me?

INITIAL READING:

_____
_____
_____

DAY'S REFLECTION:

_____
_____

TODAY'S CARD: _____

DATE: //

QUESTION: _____
_____

or choose: _____

What do I need to know today?   How can I improve today?
Where should I focus my energy?   Who is affecting me?

INITIAL READING:

_____
_____
_____

DAY'S REFLECTION:

_____
_____

TODAY'S CARD: _____

DATE: __/__/__

QUESTION: _____

or choose: _____

What do I need to know today?   How can I improve today?
Where should I focus my energy?   Who is affecting me?

INITIAL READING:

_____

_____

_____

DAY'S REFLECTION:

_____

_____

TODAY'S CARD: _____

DATE: __/__/__

QUESTION: _____

or choose:

What do I need to know today? How can I improve today?
Where should I focus my energy? Who is affecting me?

INITIAL READING:

_____

_____

_____

DAY'S REFLECTION:

_____

_____

TODAY'S CARD: _____ DATE: / /

QUESTION: _____

or choose: _____

What do I need to know today? How can I improve today?
Where should I focus my energy? Who is affecting me?

INITIAL READING:

_____
_____
_____

DAY'S REFLECTION:

_____
_____

TODAY'S CARD: _____

DATE: _/_/_

QUESTION: _____

or choose: _____

What do I need to know today?   How can I improve today?
Where should I focus my energy?   Who is affecting me?

INITIAL READING:

_____

_____

_____

DAY'S REFLECTION:

_____

_____

TODAY'S CARD: _____

DATE: / /

QUESTION: _____

or choose: _____

What do I need to know today?   How can I improve today?

Where should I focus my energy?   Who is affecting me?

INITIAL READING:

_____

_____

_____

DAY'S REFLECTION:

_____

_____

TODAY'S CARD: _____

DATE: __/__/__

QUESTION: _____

or choose: _____

What do I need to know today?   How can I improve today?
Where should I focus my energy?   Who is affecting me?

INITIAL READING:

_____
_____
_____

DAY'S REFLECTION:

_____
_____

TODAY'S CARD: _____

DATE: _/_/_

QUESTION: _____

or choose:

What do I need to know today?   How can I improve today?
Where should I focus my energy?   Who is affecting me?

INITIAL READING:

_____
_____
_____

DAY'S REFLECTION:

_____
_____

TODAY'S CARD: _____

DATE: / /

QUESTION: _____

or choose: _____

What do I need to know today?   How can I improve today?
Where should I focus my energy?   Who is affecting me?

INITIAL READING:

_____

_____

_____

DAY'S REFLECTION:

_____

_____

TODAY'S CARD: _____

DATE: / /

QUESTION: _____
_____

or choose:

What do I need to know today?   How can I improve today?
Where should I focus my energy?   Who is affecting me?

INITIAL READING:

_____
_____
_____

DAY'S REFLECTION:

_____
_____

TODAY'S CARD: _____

DATE: / /

QUESTION: _____

or choose: _____

What do I need to know today? How can I improve today?
Where should I focus my energy? Who is affecting me?

INITIAL READING:

_____
_____

DAY'S REFLECTION:

_____
_____

TODAY'S CARD: _____

DATE: _/_/_

QUESTION: _____

or choose: _____

What do I need to know today?   How can I improve today?
Where should I focus my energy?   Who is affecting me?

INITIAL READING:

_____
_____
_____

DAY'S REFLECTION:

_____
_____

TODAY'S CARD: _____

DATE: __/__

QUESTION: _____

or choose: _____

What do I need to know today?   How can I improve today?
Where should I focus my energy?   Who is affecting me?

INITIAL READING:

_____

_____

DAY'S REFLECTION:

_____

_____

TODAY'S CARD: _____

DATE: __/__

QUESTION: _____

or choose: _____

What do I need to know today?   How can I improve today?
Where should I focus my energy?   Who is affecting me?

INITIAL READING:

_____
_____
_____

DAY'S REFLECTION:

_____
_____

TODAY'S CARD: _____

DATE: _/_/_

QUESTION: _____

or choose:

What do I need to know today?   How can I improve today?
Where should I focus my energy?   Who is affecting me?

INITIAL READING:

_____

_____

_____

DAY'S REFLECTION:

_____

_____

TODAY'S CARD: _____

DATE: _/_/_

QUESTION: _____

or choose: _____

What do I need to know today?   How can I improve today?
Where should I focus my energy?   Who is affecting me?

INITIAL READING:

_____
_____
_____

DAY'S REFLECTION:

_____
_____

TODAY'S CARD: _____

DATE: __/__/__

QUESTION: _____

or choose:

What do I need to know today?   How can I improve today?
Where should I focus my energy? Who is affecting me?

INITIAL READING:

_____
_____
_____

DAY'S REFLECTION:

_____
_____

TODAY'S CARD: _____

DATE: __/__/__

QUESTION: _____

or choose: _____

What do I need to know today?   How can I improve today?
Where should I focus my energy?   Who is affecting me?

INITIAL READING:

_____
_____
_____

DAY'S REFLECTION:

_____
_____

TODAY'S CARD: _____

DATE: __/__/__

QUESTION: _____

or choose: _____

What do I need to know today?   How can I improve today?
Where should I focus my energy? Who is affecting me?

INITIAL READING:

_____

_____

_____

DAY'S REFLECTION:

_____

_____

TODAY'S CARD: _____

DATE: __/__/__

QUESTION: _____

or choose:

What do I need to know today?   How can I improve today?
Where should I focus my energy?   Who is affecting me?

INITIAL READING:

_____
_____
_____

DAY'S REFLECTION:

_____
_____

TODAY'S CARD: _____

DATE: __/__

QUESTION: _____

or choose: _____

What do I need to know today?   How can I improve today?
Where should I focus my energy?   Who is affecting me?

INITIAL READING:

_____
_____
_____

DAY'S REFLECTION:

_____
_____

TODAY'S CARD: _____

DATE: / /

QUESTION: _____

or choose: _____

What do I need to know today? How can I improve today?
Where should I focus my energy? Who is affecting me?

INITIAL READING:

_____
_____
_____

DAY'S REFLECTION:

_____

TODAY'S CARD: _____

DATE: / /

QUESTION: _____

or choose: _____

What do I need to know today?   How can I improve today?
Where should I focus my energy?   Who is affecting me?

INITIAL READING:

_____
_____
_____

DAY'S REFLECTION:

_____
_____

TODAY'S CARD: _____

DATE: _/_/_

QUESTION: _____

or choose: _____

What do I need to know today?   How can I improve today?
Where should I focus my energy?   Who is affecting me?

INITIAL READING:

_____
_____
_____

DAY'S REFLECTION:

_____
_____

TODAY'S CARD: _____

DATE: / /

QUESTION: _____

or choose: _____

What do I need to know today? How can I improve today?
Where should I focus my energy? Who is affecting me?

INITIAL READING:

_____
_____
_____

DAY'S REFLECTION:

_____
_____

TODAY'S CARD: _____

DATE: _/_/_

QUESTION: _____

or choose: _____

What do I need to know today?   How can I improve today?
Where should I focus my energy?   Who is affecting me?

INITIAL READING:

_____
_____
_____

DAY'S REFLECTION:

_____

TODAY'S CARD: _____

DATE: __/__/__

QUESTION: _____

or choose:

What do I need to know today?   How can I improve today?
Where should I focus my energy?   Who is affecting me?

INITIAL READING:

_____
_____
_____

DAY'S REFLECTION:

_____
_____

TODAY'S CARD:

DATE: / /

QUESTION:

or choose:

What do I need to know today?   How can I improve today?
Where should I focus my energy?   Who is affecting me?

INITIAL READING:

_____

_____

_____

DAY'S REFLECTION:

_____

_____

TODAY'S CARD: _____

DATE: __/__/__

QUESTION: _____

or choose:

What do I need to know today?   How can I improve today?
Where should I focus my energy?   Who is affecting me?

INITIAL READING:

_____
_____
_____

DAY'S REFLECTION:

_____
_____
_____

TODAY'S CARD: _____

DATE: __/__/__

QUESTION: _____

or choose:

What do I need to know today? How can I improve today?
Where should I focus my energy? Who is affecting me?

INITIAL READING:

_____
_____
_____

DAY'S REFLECTION:

_____
_____

TODAY'S CARD: _____

DATE: _/_/_

QUESTION: _____

or choose: _____

What do I need to know today?   How can I improve today?
Where should I focus my energy?   Who is affecting me?

INITIAL READING:

_____
_____
_____

DAY'S REFLECTION:

_____
_____

TODAY'S CARD: _____

DATE: __/__

QUESTION: _____

or choose:

What do I need to know today?   How can I improve today?
Where should I focus my energy?   Who is affecting me?

INITIAL READING:

_____
_____
_____

DAY'S REFLECTION:

_____
_____

TODAY'S CARD: _____

DATE: __/__

QUESTION: _____

or choose: _____

What do I need to know today?   How can I improve today?
Where should I focus my energy?   Who is affecting me?

INITIAL READING:

_____
_____
_____

DAY'S REFLECTION:

_____
_____

TODAY'S CARD: _____

DATE: __/__/__

QUESTION: _____

or choose: _____

What do I need to know today?   How can I improve today?
Where should I focus my energy?   Who is affecting me?

INITIAL READING:

_____
_____
_____

DAY'S REFLECTION:

_____
_____

TODAY'S CARD: _____

DATE: _/_/_

QUESTION: _____

or choose: _____

What do I need to know today? How can I improve today?
Where should I focus my energy? Who is affecting me?

INITIAL READING:

_____
_____
_____

DAY'S REFLECTION:

_____
_____

TODAY'S CARD: _____

DATE: __/__

QUESTION: _____

or choose: _____

What do I need to know today?   How can I improve today?
Where should I focus my energy?   Who is affecting me?

INITIAL READING:

_____
_____
_____

DAY'S REFLECTION:

_____
_____

TODAY'S CARD: _____

DATE: __/__/__

QUESTION: _____

or choose: _____

What do I need to know today?   How can I improve today?
Where should I focus my energy?   Who is affecting me?

INITIAL READING:

_____
_____
_____

DAY'S REFLECTION:

_____
_____

TODAY'S CARD: _____

DATE: __/__/__

QUESTION: _____

or
choose: _____

What do I need to know today?   How can I improve today?
Where should I focus my energy?   Who is affecting me?

INITIAL READING:

_____
_____
_____

DAY'S REFLECTION:

_____
_____

TODAY'S CARD: _____

DATE: __/__

QUESTION: _____

or choose: _____

What do I need to know today?   How can I improve today?
Where should I focus my energy?   Who is affecting me?

INITIAL READING:

_____
_____
_____

DAY'S REFLECTION:

_____
_____

TODAY'S CARD: _____

DATE: __/__/__

QUESTION: _____

or choose: _____

What do I need to know today?   How can I improve today?
Where should I focus my energy?   Who is affecting me?

INITIAL READING:

_____
_____
_____

DAY'S REFLECTION:

_____
_____

TODAY'S CARD: _____

DATE: / /

QUESTION: _____

or choose: _____

What do I need to know today? How can I improve today?
Where should I focus my energy? Who is affecting me?

INITIAL READING:

_____
_____

_____

DAY'S REFLECTION:

_____
_____

…
TODAY'S CARD: _____

DATE: _/_/_

QUESTION: _____

or choose: _____

What do I need to know today?   How can I improve today?
Where should I focus my energy?   Who is affecting me?

INITIAL READING:

_____
_____
_____

DAY'S REFLECTION:

_____
_____

TODAY'S CARD: _____

DATE: / /

QUESTION: _____

or choose: _____

What do I need to know today?
Where should I focus my energy?
How can I improve today?
Who is affecting me?

INITIAL READING:

_____
_____
_____

DAY'S REFLECTION:

_____
_____

TODAY'S CARD: _____

DATE: / /

QUESTION: _____
_____

or choose:
- What do I need to know today?
- Where should I focus my energy?
- How can I improve today?
- Who is affecting me?

INITIAL READING:

_____
_____
_____

DAY'S REFLECTION:

_____
_____

TODAY'S CARD: _____

DATE: __/__/__

QUESTION: _____

or choose:

What do I need to know today?
Where should I focus my energy?
How can I improve today?
Who is affecting me?

INITIAL READING:

_____
_____
_____

DAY'S REFLECTION:

_____
_____

TODAY'S CARD: _____

DATE: __/__/__

QUESTION: _____

or choose: _____

What do I need to know today?   How can I improve today?
Where should I focus my energy?   Who is affecting me?

INITIAL READING:

_____
_____
_____

DAY'S REFLECTION:

_____
_____

TODAY'S CARD:

DATE: / /

QUESTION:

or choose:

What do I need to know today?   How can I improve today?
Where should I focus my energy?   Who is affecting me?

INITIAL READING:

___

___

___

DAY'S REFLECTION:

___

___

TODAY'S CARD: _____

DATE: _/_/_

QUESTION: _____

or choose: _____

- What do I need to know today?
- Where should I focus my energy?
- How can I improve today?
- Who is affecting me?

INITIAL READING:

_____

_____

_____

DAY'S REFLECTION:

_____

_____

TODAY'S CARD: _____

DATE: _/_/_

QUESTION: _____

or choose: _____

What do I need to know today?   How can I improve today?
Where should I focus my energy?   Who is affecting me?

INITIAL READING:

_____

_____

_____

DAY'S REFLECTION:

_____

_____

TODAY'S CARD: _____

DATE: __/__

QUESTION: _____

or
choose: _____

What do I need to know today?   How can I improve today?
Where should I focus my energy?   Who is affecting me?

INITIAL READING:

_____
_____
_____

DAY'S REFLECTION:

_____
_____

TODAY'S CARD: _____

DATE: __/__

QUESTION: _____

or choose: _____

What do I need to know today?   How can I improve today?
Where should I focus my energy?   Who is affecting me?

INITIAL READING:

_____
_____
_____

DAY'S REFLECTION:

_____
_____

TODAY'S CARD:

DATE: _/_/_

QUESTION: _____

or
choose: _____

What do I need to know today?   How can I improve today?
Where should I focus my energy?   Who is affecting me?

INITIAL READING:

_____
_____
_____

DAY'S REFLECTION:

_____
_____

TODAY'S CARD: _____

DATE: __/__/__

QUESTION: _____

or choose: _____

What do I need to know today?   How can I improve today?
Where should I focus my energy?   Who is affecting me?

INITIAL READING:

_____
_____
_____

DAY'S REFLECTION:

_____
_____
_____

TODAY'S CARD: _____

DATE: __/__/__

QUESTION: _____

or
choose: _____

What do I need to know today?   How can I improve today?
Where should I focus my energy? Who is affecting me?

INITIAL READING:

_____
_____
_____

DAY'S REFLECTION:

_____
_____

TODAY'S CARD: _____

DATE: _/_/_

QUESTION: _____
_____

or choose: _____

What do I need to know today?   How can I improve today?
Where should I focus my energy?   Who is affecting me?

INITIAL READING:

_____
_____
_____

DAY'S REFLECTION:

_____
_____

TODAY'S CARD: _____

QUESTION: _____

or choose: _____

What do I need to know today?   How can I improve today?
Where should I focus my energy?   Who is affecting me?

DATE: __/__/__

INITIAL READING:

_____

_____

_____

DAY'S REFLECTION:

_____

_____

TODAY'S CARD: _____

DATE: _/_/_

Question: _____

or choose: _____

What do I need to know today?   How can I improve today?
Where should I focus my energy? Who is affecting me?

Initial Reading:

_____
_____
_____

Day's Reflection:

_____
_____

TODAY'S CARD: _____

DATE: __/__/__

QUESTION: _____

or choose: _____

What do I need to know today?   How can I improve today?
Where should I focus my energy?   Who is affecting me?

INITIAL READING:

_____
_____
_____

DAY'S REFLECTION:

_____
_____

TODAY'S CARD: _____

DATE: //

QUESTION: _____
_____

or choose:

What do I need to know today?   How can I improve today?
Where should I focus my energy? Who is affecting me?

INITIAL READING:

_____

_____

_____

DAY'S REFLECTION:

_____

_____

_____

TODAY'S CARD: _____

DATE: __/__/__

QUESTION: _____

or choose:
What do I need to know today?   How can I improve today?
Where should I focus my energy?   Who is affecting me?

INITIAL READING:

_____
_____
_____

DAY'S REFLECTION:

_____
_____

TODAY'S CARD: _____

DATE: / /

QUESTION: _____

or choose: _____

What do I need to know today?   How can I improve today?
Where should I focus my energy?   Who is affecting me?

INITIAL READING:

_____
_____
_____

DAY'S REFLECTION:

_____
_____

TODAY'S CARD: _____

DATE: __/__/__

QUESTION: _____

or
choose: _____

What do I need to know today?   How can I improve today?
Where should I focus my energy?   Who is affecting me?

INITIAL READING:

_____
_____
_____

DAY'S REFLECTION:

_____
_____

TODAY'S CARD:

DATE: / /

QUESTION: _____

or choose:

What do I need to know today?   How can I improve today?
Where should I focus my energy?   Who is affecting me?

INITIAL READING:

_____
_____
_____

DAY'S REFLECTION:

_____
_____

TODAY'S CARD: _____

DATE: __/__/__

QUESTION: _____

or choose: _____

What do I need to know today?   How can I improve today?
Where should I focus my energy?   Who is affecting me?

INITIAL READING:

_____
_____
_____

DAY'S REFLECTION:

_____
_____

TODAY'S CARD: _____

DATE: __/__

QUESTION: _____

or choose:

What do I need to know today? How can I improve today?
Where should I focus my energy? Who is affecting me?

INITIAL READING:

_____

_____

_____

DAY'S REFLECTION:

_____

_____

TODAY'S CARD: _____

DATE: _/_/_

QUESTION: _____

or choose: _____

What do I need to know today?   How can I improve today?
Where should I focus my energy?   Who is affecting me?

INITIAL READING:

_____

_____

_____

DAY'S REFLECTION:

_____

_____

TODAY'S CARD: _____

DATE: / /

QUESTION: _____

or choose: _____

What do I need to know today?   How can I improve today?
Where should I focus my energy? Who is affecting me?

INITIAL READING:

_____
_____
_____

DAY'S REFLECTION:

_____
_____

TODAY'S CARD: _____

DATE: __/__/__

QUESTION: _____

or choose: _____

What do I need to know today?   How can I improve today?
Where should I focus my energy?   Who is affecting me?

INITIAL READING:

_____
_____
_____

DAY'S REFLECTION:

_____
_____

TODAY'S CARD: _____

DATE: / /

QUESTION: _____

or choose: _____

What do I need to know today?   How can I improve today?
Where should I focus my energy?   Who is affecting me?

INITIAL READING:

_____
_____
_____

DAY'S REFLECTION:

_____
_____

TODAY'S CARD: _____

QUESTION: _____

or choose: _____

What do I need to know today?   How can I improve today?
Where should I focus my energy?   Who is affecting me?

INITIAL READING:

_____
_____
_____

DAY'S REFLECTION:

_____
_____

DATE: _/_/_

TODAY'S CARD: _____

DATE: _/_/_

QUESTION: _____

or choose: _____

What do I need to know today?   How can I improve today?
Where should I focus my energy?   Who is affecting me?

INITIAL READING:

_____
_____
_____

DAY'S REFLECTION:

_____
_____

Made in the USA
Middletown, DE
28 January 2026